W.R Sorley

# Mining royalties, and their effect on the iron and coal trades

report of an inquiry made for the Toynbee trustees

W.R Sorley

**Mining royalties, and their effect on the iron and coal trades**
*report of an inquiry made for the Toynbee trustees*

ISBN/EAN: 9783337374365

Printed in Europe, USA, Canada, Australia, Japan

Cover: Foto ©ninafisch / pixelio.de

More available books at **www.hansebooks.com**

# MINING ROYALTIES

· AND THEIR

## EFFECT ON THE IRON AND COAL TRADES

*REPORT OF AN INQUIRY MADE FOR*
*THE TOYNBEE TRUSTEES*

BY

## W. R. SORLEY, M.A.

FELLOW OF TRINITY COLLEGE, CAMBRIDGE
PROFESSOR OF PHILOSOPHY IN UNIVERSITY COLLEGE, CARDIFF
EXAMINER IN PHILOSOPHY AND POLITICAL ECONOMY
IN THE VICTORIA UNIVERSITY

London

HENRY FROWDE

OXFORD UNIVERSITY PRESS WAREHOUSE

AMEN CORNER, E.C.

1889

# CONTENTS.

———◆———

# THE TOYNBEE TRUST.

# PREFACE.

THIS Report forms one of a series of publications on English industrial matters, to be issued from time to time by the Toynbee Trustees. The objects which the Trustees had in view in the memorial they have raised to Arnold Toynbee are explained in a letter quoted in Professor Marshall's preface to Mr. Price's 'Industrial Peace.'

'What finally decided us to choose the present form of the Trust was the desire to connect the memorial both with the study of political economy in its social aspects, to which he devoted the scholar-half of himself, and with his work among the artisan population of our great cities to which he gave the other, the missionary-half. These two characters, so inextricably blended in his disposition, his scheme of life, and his actual performance, and at the same time so characteristic of what is best in the social movement of our time among the educated classes, we hoped to commemorate by a series of lectures, to be delivered not at one place, but alternately at different great industrial centres, wherever there might seem to be a real demand for them—lectures dealing with political economy on its social side, at once instructive and inspiring. They were to be, if I might use the phrase, *pioneer* lectures, breaking open the road in different places, along which others, if there was interest shown and zeal to turn that interest to good account, might subsequently march. The lecturers were to be the forerunners of the university extension movement in political economy, teaching it, always, in Toynbee's spirit; and in sending them out we hoped to benefit both the industrial centres, which they were to visit and to enrich with the learning of the university, and the university itself, to which they would return strengthened by that experience and touch with actual life, the flesh and blood of economics, which could be gained nowhere else so well as in the industrial centres. The lecturer was thus to be both a teacher and a learner, bringing back fresh knowledge of a new kind to the seat of learning, in exchange for that which he had taken with him, or rather bringing back his old knowledge mellowed by experience. Hence the provision, which is an essential part of our scheme, that the lecturer shall not be overwhelmed with teaching and class-work, but shall be so amply supplied with means and with leisure as to be able to make a fresh contribution to economic science in the shape of a special study of some point illustrated by the industrial life of the particular community in which he teaches.'[1]

The inquiry, of which the results are now published, was begun during a fifteen weeks' residence at Middlesborough in the autumn of 1887. At the request of the Toynbee Trustees, I had undertaken to lecture at a group of towns in the neighbourhood, and, at the same time, to investigate some leading feature of the mining industry of the district. After some hesitation, I decided to inquire into the effects of Mining Royalties. The pressure of a fixed charge on production was keenly felt at the time, owing to the long-continued depression of trade ; and it therefore seemed important to ascertain the exact way in which royalty-charges are connected with prices and with the conditions of employment. No full statistics of the amount of royalties were obtainable. The conditions of mining leases are matters of private arrangement between landlord and employer, and do not attain the publicity which belongs to all the transactions of the employer with his workmen in fixing wages, and with the consumers in determining prices. But, through the kind offices of several friends, I was put in possession of a considerable number of facts bearing on the royalty question. This material, gathered on the spot in Cleveland, was afterwards supplemented by inquiries in other districts, and from published sources. Complete statistical detail is still wanting, and would undoubtedly be valuable. But the facts collected are, I believe, full and varied enough to check theoretical deductions, and to form the basis of an economic argument.

I have judged it better to withhold the names of my authorities for unpublished facts. In some cases, this was made a condition

---

[1] Quoted in Professor Marshall's preface to Mr. Price's 'Industrial Peace' (Macmillan, 1887).

of my receiving information. But I wish to take this opportunity of expressing my obligations to those friends who have assisted me in carrying out and completing the inquiry: especially to Professor Foxwell, Dr. Spence Watson, and Mr. Aneurin Williams.

My thanks are also due to the Council of the Royal Statistical Society, both for giving the following pages a place in the *Journal* of the Society (March, 1889), and for allowing their re-publication in the present form.

Parts of the present paper were read to the Economic Section of the British Association for the Advancement of Science, at the Bath Meeting, 1888, and an abstract of it is published in the *Report* of the Association.

W. R. SORLEY.

UNIVERSITY COLLEGE, CARDIFF,
April, 1889.

# MINING ROYALTIES.

## I.—*Historical.*

THE origin of property in mines, and of the royalties and other dues paid by the mine worker to the landlord, is involved in considerable obscurity. We are however able to enumerate the chief causes which have brought about the present state of the ownership of minerals in this country, though it is more difficult to trace the operation of these causes, and show how they combined to produce the result. The causes referred to seem to have been, in the main, these four: In the first place, the Roman law regulating property in land and mines, as subsequently modified by feudal ideas, and adopted in England; secondly, the customs (themselves sufficiently obscure in origin) which ruled in certain mining districts anterior to any statute law; thirdly, encroachments upon customary rights, similar to those which brought about the enclosure of commons; and, in the last place, the exclusive right claimed by the Crown to gold and silver and the minerals containing them.

In the Roman law we find both the assertion of Crown rights to minerals, and the admission, under certain conditions, of property in them as belonging to the owner of the surface. The seigneurial rights claimed by the Roman emperors over all lands whatever extended also to mines. The subject was, at most, the *dominus uti* or beneficial owner of mines as of the soil; and from both a revenue might be raised for the State. In conquered countries, moreover, the Roman State succeeded to the status and rights of the conquered government, and thus, in countries such as Spain and Macedonia, obtained exclusive property (*i.e., dominium utile* as well as *dominium strictum*) in the mines of gold and silver. A claim to the exclusive possession of all minerals whatever was even made by Tiberius. But the more moderate claim of the

Emperor Gratian (367-83 A.D.) was that which became the final measure of imperial mining rights. The claim thus made asserted first, the exclusive right to the full legal and beneficial ownership of all gold and silver mines; and secondly, the right to receive a proportion of the produce of all other mines. This proportion was usually one-tenth, payable by the actual mine worker to the Crown directly. If the mine worker was also the owner (*i.e.*, occupant) of the lands, he was owner also of the minerals subject only to such payment. If the mine worker was not the owner of the lands, then he had further to pay to the latter one-tenth of the produce: subject to the payment of such two equal tenth parts, the mine worker was the owner of the minerals.[1]

What is noticeable here, in addition to the assertion of the Crown's right to a royalty on the output, is the limitation of the claim possessed by the (beneficial) owner of the soil to the ownership of the minerals. The necessity must have been early felt of regulating the conditions under which mines should be worked by others than the occupants of the surface. And by this regulation, they became the property of the worker, subject to the payment of a fixed part of the produce to the owner of the soil, and a similar payment to the Crown.

To these regulations we may trace, if we please, the royal claim to minerals in England, the landlord's property in mines, and the royalty system. There is no good ground however for referring either to Roman law, or to the grant of the sovereign, the various local customs which regulated the early right of mining in this and many other countries, and which, at later periods, were confirmed or modified by statute law. The opinion of Mr. Bainbridge, indeed, seems to be that they were derived from the concession of crown rights. Speaking of the customary law of the lead mines of Derbyshire, he says:—

"It would be difficult to trace with accuracy the origin and " growth of those peculiar customs, but they may probably be " most correctly regarded as rights of the Crown, which were " from time to time expressly or impliedly conceded by the Crown " to the people of the country, and either subject or not subject " to certain renders to the Crown. Almost all the old mining " codes of Europe whose provisions are opposed to the rights of " the owner of the surface, must have originated in the old " Roman law, or in the royal prerogative, or in the successful " assertion of high feudal privileges."[2]

For this view, stated with growing confidence as the paragraph proceeds, there does not seem to be sufficient evidence. The local

---

[1] Bainbridge, "Law of Mines and Minerals," chap. vi, sec. 1, 4th edit., 1878.
[2] "Law of Mines and Minerals," p. 138.

customs referred to survive, in modified form, in this country in the Forest of Dean and parts of Cornwall, Devon, Derbyshire, and Wales. In spite of much divergency of detail they all seem to have sprung from a condition of affairs in which mining was free. Anyone who would—the first discoverer—usually had the right of marking out and working a certain area or certain lode, provided he conformed to the rules imposed by the local authorities. Similar rights existed in ancient and mediæval Germany ; and the American mining customs, founded on the practice of the Spanish miners, betray similar characteristics. This freedom of mining (*Bergbaufreiheit*), or right of anyone to work mines in his own or another's ground, has, with great probability, been connected with the original common ownership and common use of the mark.[3] The mining privileges of various districts were not derived, as Bainbridge supposes, from the royal concession of Crown rights to the people. On the contrary, the local customs now existing, so far as they indicate free mining, are in all likelihood the remnants of a widely extended condition of affairs which has been everywhere transformed, and, in most districts, entirely superseded, by the extension of the royal prerogative and of feudal tenure, and by the encroachments of private proprietors.

Traces of the operation of this last cause may be found in the modern Enclosure Acts, in which the right to the mines is reserved to the lord of the manor. The spirit of English law is hostile to the older system of common property ; and the gradual disappearance of common rights in the soil and the monopoly by the strongest member of the community of its property as his individual possession, which have been so frequently manifested in the changes of the ownership of the surface, seem to have been operative in the case of the ownership of minerals as well ; until, except in a few localities, in which the customary rights were never allowed to lapse altogether, the minerals under the soil came to be regarded as the private property of the owner of the surface, in the absence of express evidence to the contrary. This, indeed, is a maxim of English law : *cujus est solum, ejus est usque at cœlum, et deinde usque ad inferos.*

The rights of the Crown, equally with the rights of the people, have gradually disappeared before those of the private proprietors. The rights claimed by the English Crown were at first extensive. " But in these early times," says Bainbridge,[4] " the mines of tin " and lead and of gold and silver were, if not the only, at least " the principal, mines to which industry was directed ; and by the

---

[3] Leuthold, Art. " Bergrecht," in Holtzendorff's " Rechtslexicon," 3te Aufl., I, 286.

[4] " Law of Mines and Minerals," chap. vi, sec. 2.

" time that industry began to extend itself to mines of coal, iron,
" and such like other baser substances, the spirit of liberty and of
" private encroachment, fostered and protected by the genius as
" well as by the forms of English law, occasioned the assertion by
" individual landowners of rights that were exclusive of the Crown.
" Whence it appears that in or about the year 1568, the respective
" adverse rights of the Crown and of private landowners became
" the subject of contention, and called for definition by the courts
" of justice." The decision of the judges in this so-called "great
" case of mines" (Queen *v.* Northumberland) was in effect "that
" only the so-called royal mines [*i.e.*, those of gold or silver]
" belonged to the Crown, and that all the baser minerals belonged
" to the individual landowner." This decision carried with it the
right of the Crown to search for gold or silver: to enter upon
private land, and carry on the operations necessary for obtaining
the precious metals. The judges who decided the case further
held (by a majority) that a mine of baser metal, if it contained
*any* gold or silver, was a royal mine. But as gold and silver,
when found in this country, are almost always found along with
other metals, and as it was a prevalent superstition at the time
that all other metals contain them,[5] this decision might have
admitted of an indefinite extension of the Crown rights. The
uncertainty to which it gave rise, and which was found to interfere seriously with mining industry, was ultimately set at rest by
statutes,[6] which confirmed the private ownership of mines containing copper, tin, iron, or lead (notwithstanding their being
claimed to be royal mines), subject to a right of pre-emption of
the minerals by the Crown. As the prices fixed for the Crown's
pre-emption have, in nearly every case, exceeded the selling price
of the minerals since the passing of the Acts, the danger of royal
interference, which had, at one time, been a serious obstacle to the
working of minerals, ceased to exist. All minerals (except gold
and silver) have thus in England come to be recognised as private
property as much as land; and the recent case at Dolgelly in
North Wales shows that the Crown rights to gold and silver,
though still maintained, are assessed in such a way as not to
interfere with the stimulus to private enterprise.[7]

Up to a certain time the question as to the possession of
minerals on the continent of Europe seems to have been subject

---

[5] *Cf.* Hunt, "British Mining," p. 127, 2nd edit., 1887.

[6] 3 William and Mary, cap. 30; 5 William and Mary, cap. 6; 55 Geo. III,
cap. 134.

[7] The royalty agreed upon is understood to be one-thirtieth of the output (see
"Western Mail" for 30th May, 20th June, and 8th October, 1888); and
Mr. Pritchard Morgan allows that "the Government was dealing with the whole
"question in a very fair and liberal spirit" ("Western Mail," 21st May, 1888").

to similar influences to those operative in this country. But the development of the law on the subject in every important mining country except Russia and England, was turned into a new direction by the influence, direct or indirect, of the French mining legislation of 1789 and 1810. According to the latter law, which re-enacts the main provisions of that of 1789, minerals do not belong to the owner of the surface, or to anyone until conceded by the State. A State concession of minerals creates a new property different from and independent of that of the surface, and capable of transference like other properties. The system, it is to be noted, is not the same thing as one of State ownership. The mine belongs to no one until conceded by the State, or is only in the nominal possession of the State, which never works it itself nor lets it at a competitive rent. When conceded to anyone it belongs to the *concessionaire* as absolutely as any other property does.[8] At the same time, the State may and commonly does exact, in return for the concession, certain dues from the *concessionaire* in the form of initial payment, rent, or royalty. These payments differ considerably in different countries and different districts, and in different circumstances in the same country. But, subject to these charges, and with some differences of legal technicality, the ownership of minerals is vested in the State *concessionaire* in France, Germany, Belgium, Spain, Portugal, Sweden, Norway, and the greater part of Italy (namely, Sardinia and all upper and central Italy with the exception of the Tuscan provinces).

It has been already pointed out that, according to the claim made by the Emperor Gratian, the mine worker had to pay to the State one-tenth of the produce of the mine, and that a payment of the same amount had to be made by him to the landlord, if he was : not himself the owner (occupant) of the surface. The payment thus agreed in nature with the modern royalty. It rose and fell with the produce of the mine. But the earliest mineral leases in this country do not seem to have been of the same nature. Mr. Galloway, in his " History of Coal Mining,"[9] says that, " in the " earliest leases of which we find mention (such as those granted " by the monks of Tynemouth about 1330 A.D.) a certain rent per " annum was alone reserved by the lessors, without any stipulation " as to the quantity of coal allowed to be worked for the same. " But the necessity of making the quantity of coal drawn from " the mine bear a fixed relation to the amount of rent paid,

---

[8] In some cases, however, the concession is limited. According to the law of Napoleon (of 9th August, 1808), in force in the Italian provinces of Modena and Reggio, concessions "are not granted for ever, but only for a term not exceeding " fifty years, subject to renewal."—" Reports on Mining Rents and Royalties, " Commercial," No. 7 (1887), p. 21.

[9] London, 1882, p. 17.

" soon became felt, and as early as the middle of the fourteenth
" century provisions were introduced for this purpose. At first this
" was effected by simply limiting the quantity of coal which might
" be worked. Thus in a lease of five mines at Whickham, made by
" the Bishop of Durham in 1356, it was stipulated that the lessees
" might not draw from each mine more than *one keel* (21 tons) per
" day. The arrangement of limiting the quantity of coal to be
" worked was the plan usually adopted in leases, until the introduc-
" tion of the more improved modern method of having both a fixed
" and a sliding, or tonnage rent, which makes the amount of rent
" to be in exact proportion to the quantity of coal worked." The
modern method, however, seems to have been long in being
universally adopted. Thus in 1748 the then Marquis of Bute
leased extensive tracts of ironstone and coal fields (for ninety-nine
or for a hundred years) to the firm now represented by the Dowlais
Company, for the certain rent only of 100*l.* a year. After this
lease had expired it was renewed on the royalty system, after
prolonged and disastrous contention between the contracting
parties. To show the superiority (from the landlord's point of
view) of the modern method of assessment, it may be added that
the amount actually paid to the landlord in the first year of the
new lease was (if my information is correct) 20,000*l.*, as against
100*l.* for each year under the old lease.

## II.—*Descriptive.*

The payments made by the mine workers to the landlord in
this country consist of: (1) a fixed or certain or dead rent, (2) a
royalty or payment per ton of mineral worked, (3) in some cases,
payments for instroke or outstroke, shaft, and wayleave.

(1.) Certain or dead rent :—

When a mine is leased, the landlord stipulates for a certain
annual payment whatever quantity of mineral be worked, or even
if the mine be allowed to stand idle; otherwise his mine might
be allowed to remain unworked through the mismanagement of
the lessee, and the landlord be unable to obtain any income from
his property. The certain rent is not charged in addition to the
royalty payment. If the certain rent be 1,000*l.* and the royalty
6*d.*, the first 40,000 tons worked in any year pay no royalty. Should
less than 40,000 tons be worked, 1,000*l.* must still be paid. But a
clause in the lease usually admits of such short workings, or
" shorts," being recovered, *i.e.*, worked without additional royalty
payment in some subsequent year. Sometimes shorts must be
worked in the next year, sometimes in the next four or five, or ten
years, sometimes in any subsequent year of the lease. Five years
seems to be the period commonly allowed for working them. And

this restriction of the period allowed for working shorts is felt as a grievance, especially in districts such as Cleveland, where the certain rents are high. In Cleveland, and perhaps in other districts, the certain rents are calculated on the principle of being equal to the total royalty yield of the mine, divided by the number of years of the lease, the mine being generally exhausted at the end of the lease. The importance of this part of the subject may be illustrated from the evidence of Mr. A. Hewlett before the Royal Commission on the Depression of Trade and Industry. The Wigan Coal and Iron Company, with about 200 leases, has (he says) overpaid in this way about 260,000*l.*;[10] and Sir Lowthian Bell says that for this fixed payment, and for keeping the mine free from water, and the machinery, &c., in good repair, he "could name "cases in which 20,000*l.*, or 30,000*l.*, a year would not suffice."[11]

(2.) Royalties:—

In a system which admits of the possession of minerals by others than those who work them, the royalty rent finds its obvious justification in the deterioration of the mine by each quantity of mineral removed. The royalty protects the landlord against the rapid exhaustion of the mine, as the certain rent protects him against its lying idle. The royalty is nearly always estimated at so much per ton or other quantity of mineral extracted. In south Yorkshire, however, the coal field is rented by the acre, an estimate being made of the quantity of coal which the acre is likely to yield. "Sometimes it is taken by what we call footage "rent, that is to say, so much per foot, whatever thickness it runs "to it is paid for accordingly."[12] A similar method is common in south Staffordshire. The tonnage or (in Northumberland and Durham) tentail rent, is, however, much more common.

The royalties in different parts of the country vary largely with the quality of the mineral, the thickness of strata, freedom from "troubles," or faults in the strata, accessibility of markets, &c. Thus in Northumberland the present royalty on coal is usually about 4*d.* or 4½*d.* a ton, having diminished considerably of late; that in south Wales is said to be about 9*d.*[13] In south Staffordshire, according to my information, "where payment is made on "the selling price at the pit's mouth, royalties vary between one-"eighth and one-fourteenth; when by the ton, from 6*d.* to 10*d.*; "when by the foot thick per acre, from 12*l.* 10*s.* to 40*l.*, and when "per acre all prices from 150*l.* to 1,000*l.*" The Cleveland ironstone

---

[10] Report, *Q.* 12,122 and 12,123.

[11] Second Report, Appendix I, p. 75 of pamphlet.

[12] "Report of the Royal Commission on the Depression of Trade," *Q.* 3127—3134. (Evidence of Mr. J. D. Ellis, chairman of John Brown and Co., and of the South Yorkshire Coal Association.)

[13] Speech of Mr. W. Abraham, in the House of Commons, 14th May, 1886.

is spoken of as paying a normal royalty of 6*d.* or 7*d.*, but in many of the most productive mines the royalty would seem to be much less. Comparing Sir B. Samuelson's statement, quoted below, that in Cleveland the royalties in ironstone alone in 1886 amounted to more than 120,000*l.*, with the quantity of Cleveland ironstone produced in that year (5,370,279 tons), the average royalty is found to be under 5½*d.*; while for the rich hæmatite ores of Cumberland the normal royalty (according to the sliding scale arrangement in force there) is 2*s.*, and as much as 9*s.* or 10*s.* a ton royalty has been paid at the time of very high prices.[14]

(3.) Wayleaves are of two kinds, which it seems important to distinguish :—

(*a.*) When the way granted is over, or under the surface of, land which is not being mined; (*b.*) when it is through a mine which is being worked. The former requires separate consideration; the latter may be treated along with shaft instroke and outstroke rents. These latter may be dealt with first.

When a lease is taken, and the lessee sinks his shaft in the property of the lessor, neither instroke, wayleave, nor shaft rent is paid. But the same lessee may also take an adjoining royalty belonging to another owner. And it often happens, in such a case (either because the landlord objects to the surface of his property being defaced, or because the lessee is anxious to save the capital expenditure of a new shaft and buildings), that the mineral from the second royalty is brought through the first mine and up its shaft. In doing this the lessee has to pay a tonnage to the owner of the first royalty : first, for bringing the mineral through the barrier between the mines, called instroke, or from the other point of view, outstroke rent; secondly, for the wayleave from the barrier to the shaft; and thirdly, for bringing the mineral up the shaft. These items are commonly at or a little less than ½*d.* a ton each (for coal) in Durham and Northumberland. The charges for the three processes (which are really only parts of one process) are usually combined into a single payment per ton.

These payments are sometimes considered unfair and excessive. The question of their incidence will be discussed at a subsequent stage. But, for purposes of explanation, it may be as well to point out at present that a mine is deteriorated by its barrier from the surrounding property being removed. It is thereby rendered liable to be invaded by water or noxious gases from the neighbouring mine. That payment should be made for instroke or outstroke is therefore reasonable. Whether this should be in the form of a tonnage charge would seem to depend on whether the mine suffers

---

[14] "Report of the Royal Commission on the Depression of Trade," *Q.* 2313 and 2314. (Evidence of Mr. I. T. Smith.)

according to the amount of mineral brought through the barrier. But it certainly appears strange that the lessee should have to make an additional payment in the form of wayleave and shaft rent, for every ton of mineral he brings along the ways he has himself constructed, and up the shaft he has himself sunk. The answer may of course be made, and must be allowed due weight, that the matter is one which has been settled by a contract to which the lessee has agreed. If payment were not made for shaft or wayleave, so much more might be charged for instroke. Still it is deserving of notice that, in this matter, the lessee seems not to have been able to make a contract with the landlord in which each separate payment is in return for value received; and the landlord would appear to have been able to dictate his own terms.

The other kind of wayleave—that across or under ground which is not itself mined—differs in nature from the preceding. But, in this case, as in the former, the owner of the way is able to charge for it a price proportioned to the necessity of the buyer. It is evident, of course, that the tonnage charged bears no relation to value removed from the soil. The property is not deteriorated according to the amount of mineral carried. Instances are sometimes quoted of the charges for wayleave weighing so heavily as to lead to the giving up of the working of a mine, while other cases are mentioned of a mine lying unworked on account of the unwillingness of a neighbouring proprietor to grant a wayleave. This, again, is of course a matter of contract in which the individual avails himself of the advantages of his situation. A penny a ton for leave to bring mineral underneath a field 40 yards across (yielding in the case referred to some 600*l.* a year to the owner of the field), certainly appears to be an exorbitant rent, though it may be paralleled in many other cases of the " unearned increment " which a valuable monopoly may yield.

In addition to the above, which are payments for the minerals, the landlord is usually compensated by an additional payment for the use of, and injury done to, the surface. And for these he is generally able to secure favourable terms in the lease. Thus a lease of which I have had the details, and which is probably typical, gives double its agricultural value to the landlord for the use of the surface ; and the lessees further agree to restore the surface at the end of the lease, or pay the fee simple of the land to the lessor, who retains possession. Regarding the effects of this condition, I am informed by a correspondent in south Staffordshire that " the " liability to level and restore damaged surface is always cast on " the lessees, and about 30*l.* an acre is usually paid by way of com- " pensation in lieu of levelling. The lessor almost invariably puts " the money in his pocket, and leaves the land waste ; the result

" being that we have round us many thousand acres of spoil banks,
" which might be productive land, utterly waste, to the loss of
" capital, labour, local trade, and national wealth."

There are no sufficient data for determining the exact amount
of mineral rents and royalties in the United Kingdom; and as long
as secrecy is the rule of trade, it seems hopeless to look for them.
But some estimates as to particular districts, and as to the whole
kingdom, may be given. Sir B. Samuelson,[15] who has the most
accurate data to go upon, tells us that, for the thirty-seven years
from 1850 to 1886, the royalties paid on ironstone alone in the
district of Middlesborough (Cleveland) amounted to 2,900,000*l.*
In 1886 they were over 120,000*l.* The royalties paid on the coal
used in the manufacture of pig-iron for the same thirty-seven years
were 2,450,000*l.* In 1886 they amounted to over 100,000*l.* That
is to say, the royalties for coal and ironstone used in the manufacture of Cleveland pig are at present over 220,000*l.* per annum.
A more detailed estimate, depending on the same data, is given by
Mr. C. M. Percy.[16] " The royalty on Cleveland ironstone leased
" before 1870 would average 5*d.* per ton, and that leased during
" the years leading up to 1874 would average 6*d.* per ton ; but as
" Mr. Dennington [secretary of the Cleveland Mineowners' Asso-
" ciation] says, practically all the valuable ironstone in the
" Cleveland district had been leased previous to 1870. . . In
" the fourteen years ending 1863 the Cleveland annual ironstone
" output was 1,250,000 tons; in the nine years ending 1872 the
" Cleveland annual ironstone output was 3,358,000 tons; and in
" the fourteen years ending 1886, the Cleveland annual ironstone
" output was 5,941,991 tons, making a total in thirty-seven years
" of 130,909,946 tons, for which 3,000,000*l.* was paid in royalty.
" From this 40,000,000 tons of Cleveland pig-iron was made, on
" which the total amount of royalty paid on the ironstone, and the
" coal (and the limestone reckoned at 1½*d.* a ton) has been
" 6,000,000*l.*"

Mr. W. Abraham, again, says that the coal royalties in south
Wales amount annually to 600,000*l.*, taking the royalty at 9*d.* a
ton on an annual production of 16 million tons.[17] And he further
says that royalties of all kinds in the United Kingdom are com-
puted at 36 million £ a year,—on what grounds I do not know.
Mr. Percy's estimate of the whole coal royalties of the United
Kingdom is that they amount to 5,500,000*l.*, taking the average
royalty at 8*d.* on a total annual production of 160 million tons;
while as regards ironstone the average yearly production during

---

[15] "Northern Echo," 6th November, 1887.
[16] "Mine Rents and Mineral Royalties," pp. 20 and 21. Wigan, 1888.
[17] Speech in House of Commons, 14th May, 1886.

the last ten years has not been less than 16 million tons, " which
" at the very moderate estimate of 9*d.* per ton on an average,
" considerably exceeds an annual royalty payment of half a mil-
" lion of money." [18]

The estimates as to the average royalties on coal and iron ore
have been already mentioned incidentally. The royalties in different
districts, however, differ so greatly that in default of more complete
information those estimates cannot but be somewhat rough. Thus
the average royalty in south Wales on coal is probably nearly
double that in Durham and Northumberland, where the miners
are already in the region of the thin seams; and a similar difference
holds of ironstone, where the royalties ou the rich hæmatite ores of
Cumberland or on the Scotch blackband are immensely higher
than those on the poorer and phosphoric ores of Cleveland. Sir
Lowthian Bell[19] has estimated that the royalties on a ton of pig
iron for ironstone, coal, &c., amount in Cleveland to 3*s.* 6*d.*, in
Scotland to 6*s.*, and in Cumberland to 6*s.* 3*d.*, as compared with
about 6*d.* a ton paid iu Germany, 8*d.* in France, and 1*s.* 3*d.* or
1*s.* 4*d.* in Belgium. In the United States, where large tracts of
mineral land have frequently been bought up by speculators, high
competitive royalties of from 2*s.* to 3*s.* a ton are not uncommon.
The royalties seem, however, to have varied considerably of late.
Thus, Mr. I. T. Smith, of Barrow, tells the Royal Commission on
the Depression of Trade[20] that "the royalty that we pay now is
" 2*s.* a ton, but during the last year or two in the Lancashire
" district the royalties will only have been about 1*s.* 6*d.* a ton; so
" that the cost upon a ton of pig iron during the last two or three
" years has been only 4*s.* and not 6*s.*"

The following tables may present some of the above facts more
clearly. Table A is a return submitted to the House of Commons,
22nd September, 1886, showing the gross amounts payable to the
Ecclesiastical Commissioners for England in respect of royalties and
other charges on mineral property during five consecutive years.
It is the only exact and detailed account of the amount of royalties,
even within a limited district, with which I am acquainted.
Table B gives some material for a comparison of average royalties
in different districts.

[18] "Mine Rents and Mineral Royalties," pp. 20 and 21.
[19] "Principles of the Manufacture of Iron and Steel, 1884," pp. 603 and 610.
[20] Report, Q. 2443.

TABLE A.—*Amounts Payable to the Ecclesiastical Commissioners in the County of Durham.*
*Mineral Rents, Royalties, Wayleaves, &c.*

| Year Ending 31st March, | 1 Coal. | | | 2 Ironstone. | | | 3 Fire Clay. | | | 4 and 5 Limestone and Freestone. | | | 6 Lead Ore, &c. | | | 7 Wayleave and Watercourse Rents. | | | 8 Instroke, Outstroke, Shaft, and Wayleave Rents. | | |
|---|---|---|---|---|---|---|---|---|---|---|---|---|---|---|---|---|---|---|---|---|---|
| | | | | | | | | | | Amount Due. | | | | | | | | | | | |
| | £ | s. | d. | £ | s. | d | £ | s. | d. | £ | s. | d. | £ | s. | d. | £ | s. | d. | £ | s. | d. |
| 1881.... | 117,867 | 3 | 6 | 1,923 | 4 | 8 | 2,648 | 5 | – | 4,200 | 9 | 11 | 6,636 | 9 | 1 | 15,467 | 15 | 7 | 15,772 | 2 | – |
| '82.... | 125,720 | 3 | 4 | 2,117 | 11 | 8 | 2,708 | 3 | – | 4,569 | 10 | 7 | 2,624 | 6 | 2 | 15,274 | 11 | 3 | 15,168 | 1 | 11 |
| '83.... | 135,955 | 1 | 10 | 1,152 | 15 | 4 | 2,277 | 2 | 2 | 5,605 | 18 | 1 | 1,587 | 6 | 8 | 15,670 | 18 | 10 | 18,669 | 6 | 8 |
| '84... | 137,069 | 1 | 8 | 1,224 | 8 | 9 | 2,222 | 9 | 3 | 5,797 | 13 | 6 | 2,706 | 2 | 3 | 16,336 | 6 | 11 | 18,606 | 5 | 5 |
| '85.... | 141,083 | 4 | 9 | 909 | 4 | – | 2,183 | 5 | 9 | 7,224 | 15 | 7 | 1,145 | – | – | 17,023 | 15 | 9 | 18,106 | 10 | 2 |

TABLE B.—*Comparative Average Royalties in Selected Districts.*

| Coal. | Per Ton. | Ironstone. | Per Ton. | Per Ton of Pig Iron (for Ore, Coal, Limestone, &c.). |
|---|---|---|---|---|
| Northumberland and Durham ............... | 4½d.[a] | Cleveland ................ | 5½d.[d] | 3s.[f] |
| South Staffordshire .... | 6d. to 10d. | Cumberland and Lancashire ........ | 2s.[e] | 6s. 3d.[g] |
| „    Yorkshire ........ | 6d.[b] | Scotland— | | |
| Lancashire .................... | 6d.[c] | On clay band ....... | ? | 3s.[f] |
| South Wales ............... | 9d. | „   black  „   ........ | (?) 2s. | 6s.[f] |

[a] Private information, and Mr. J. B. Simpson's evidence before the Royal Commission on the Depression of Trade (Q. 12357), that royalty is about one-twelfth of selling price in Durham, and that the average selling price (Q. 12447) is 4s. 7d.

[b] Mr. J. D. Ellis's evidence before the same commission, Q. 3128.

[c] Mr. A. Hewlett's evidence, Q. 12138.

[d] Sir B. Samuelson's statement of amount of royalty paid in 1886 compared with output for that year.

[e] Mr. I. T. Smith's evidence, Q. 2313—14 and 2443.

[f] Sir L. Bell's evidence, Q. 3565.

[g] The same. Mr. I. T. Smith says 6s. 6d., Q. 2221.

III.—*Opinions of the Trade on the Incidence of Royalties.*

It may be of use at this stage to collect a few representative opinions regarding the effect of mineral royalties from those who are engaged in the iron and coal industries.

In the first place prominence should be given to the carefully weighed opinion of Sir Lowthian Bell. In the present depression, he says, "it is widely felt as a grievance that the landowners to " whom royalties are payable receive the full amount reserved by

" the leases. It is contended that should the present low prices
" continue, those engaged in mining in this country must be reduced
" to bankruptcy, and a great industry must be extinguished, unless
" the receivers of royalties are willing to abate something of their
" legal rights, which now give them about 3s. on every ton of the
" cheapest kinds of pig iron made, or very nearly 10 per cent. on
" the gross price of the manufactured article...... Even now
" the owners of minerals in the less favourably situated mines are
" forced in a losing trade to make concessions to their lessees,
" though they are able, if they hold out for their full legal rights,
" to see all the capital of the tenant made valueless, before the loss
" begins to fall on themselves in respect of the royalty......
" The injustice, as it has been termed, is remarked on, of the work-
" men having their wages reduced, and the railway companies their
" rates lowered, while the landowners remain unaffected...... It
" would seem, therefore,' he adds, " open to consideration whether,
" by means of a sliding scale the payments to the landlord should
" not be made dependent on the market value of the mineral, a
" system which in some cases has already been adopted." [21]  For
carrying out this modification he thinks that legislation need not
be appealed to. [22]

Again, Mr. Adamson, in his presidential address to the Iron
and Steel Institute, speaks of "the high royalties which have to
" be paid for minerals in England " as one of the "two great
" obstacles which stand in our way as compared with the position
" of our foreign competitors." "At present," he says, " these
" royalties are so heavy as to constitute a tax that precludes the
" chance of competing successfully with some other countries." [23]
To the same effect Mr. I. T. Smith testifies that "if we were
" paying less in royalties, we should be better able to compete with
" other countries;" [24] while Mr. J. B. Simpson remarks in his
evidence before the Royal Commission that mine owners' capital
is absorbed by royalties, just as that of farmers is absorbed by
agricultural rent. [25]

At the same time certain considerations have to be taken into
account as modifying this very decided expression of opinion.
There are especially two points in the evidence before the Royal
Commission of a witness already quoted, Mr. I. T. Smith, which
need consideration. [26]  The first point is practically this, that
royalties are high, not only because landlords wish to get, but

[21] " Second Report of the Royal Commission on the Depression of Trade,"
Appendix I, pp. 77 and 78.
[22] Report, Q. 3562.
[23] " Journal of the Iron and Steel Institute," 1887, p. 25.
[24] " Report of the Royal Commission on the Depression of Trade," Q. 2322.
[25] Ibid., Q. 12480.      [26] Q. 2318, 2358, and 2450.

because lessees are willing to give, high prices: "I have never
" known a lessor ask more than he could get from somebody.  The
" amount of royalty demanded is the amount the owner finds he
" can get if he has his property to lease. . . . . . I know that in
" foreign countries the royalties are less, but I know the conditions
" of our mines are such that if we gave them up there would be
" fifty people glad to take them at the price we are paying; there-
" fore I cannot conceive there could be any conditions by which
" the lessees, whoever they might be, could get them for any less
" amount." The second point has reference to the growing power
of foreign competition: "The expansion of the iron trade as
" referring to steel in Germany has not been a question of royalty
" during the last four or five years, so much as the discovery of a
" process by which their own ore can be converted into steel."
    It is well known that an opinion adverse to the present royalty
system is held by most representative bodies of miners.  In
answer to the question of the Royal Commissioners, "Are there
" any special circumstances affecting your district to which the
" existing condition of trade and industry therein can be attri-
" buted?" the depression is attributed (amongst nine other
causes) to "the effect of excessive royalties" in the answers from
the West Bromwich, Oldbury, Tipton, and Corely Amalgamated
Association of Miners.  The West Cumberland Miners' Association
reports still more decidedly that "high royalty rents, railway
" carriage and land monopolies prevent their district from being
" able to compete with others in several markets;" and that
" owing to the high royalty rents the iron ore trade is doing only
" about half it ought to do."[27]
    What the miners communicated to the Royal Commissioners is
proclaimed by them with greater freedom and emphasis at public
meetings.  At a meeting of the Northumberland Political Reform
Association on 17th September, 1887, a motion in favour of "the
" entire abolition of royalty rents" was carried by a small majority,
over a motion that the miners declare themselves "not in favour
" of the total abolition of royalty rents, but the abolition of
" private ownership in minerals."[28]  No other proposals than these
two, *i.e.*, abolition or regulation, free mining (in some form) or
State ownership, was even put to the meeting.  Again, at a meeting
of the South Wales Colliery Workmen's Federation on 12th June,
1888, a motion proposed by Mr. W. Abraham, M.P., was agreed to
(though not without some more extreme expressions of opinion), to
the effect "that this conference is of opinion that the royalty
" rents question demands immediate attention, with the view of

---

[27] Second Report, Appendix D, pp. 92 and 94.
[28] "Newcastle Daily Chronicle," 19th September, 1887.

" bringing about radical revision in the impost in the direction of
" diminution and regulation, so as to remove the injustice so far as
" it is an impediment upon the industry of the country."[29]

To the above expressions of opinion it must now be added that
the question of mining royalties, and of property in minerals
generally, has (since the Birmingham meeting of the National
Liberal Federation in 1888) received a place on the programme of
the Liberal party.

The objections thus made to the present royalty system may, I
think, be fairly summarised under the three following heads:—

1. That royalties being measured by a fixed sum of money per
quantity of output, weigh with exceptional severity upon the trade
whenever it is already in a depressed condition and prices are low.

2. That English trade is placed at a disadvantage, owing to
heavy royalties, in competition with foreign countries where the
royalty is low or where there is hardly any royalty.

3. That it is "unfair" or "unjust" for the landlord's rent to
continue unimpaired when the wages of workmen are being
reduced and the profits of employers disappear; and even (as is
frequently argued on platforms) that it is unjust for the landlord
to claim any right to the minerals under his land, seeing he did
not put them there.

The opinions just quoted agree at any rate in this, that the
present royalties are a burden upon English industry, and that
their modification, or even entire abolition, would contribute
towards improving the condition of trade. But there is no
general agreement as to the practical methods to be adopted
in the circumstances, nor even as to the actual incidence of the
royalty payments and their effect upon wages, profits, and price.
It seems even to be sometimes assumed that any reduction in the
amount of royalties would go directly towards the cheapening of
the raw material and manufactured goods. The large sums paid
for mineral rents and royalties are calculated or estimated, and the
industry of the country is then said to be taxed to the extent of
36 millions. How far and in what way the royalty affects the
price is a question which, so far as I am aware, has not been
investigated. It would seem better therefore to consider this
question first before dealing with various matters of detail, and
with the more complicated question of reform.

#### IV.—*The Incidence of Royalties.*

The theory of mine rents is commonly treated by economists as
an appendix to the theory of agricultural rent; and I believe this
method is in the main correct. But it is of the greatest import-

[20] "South Wales Daily News," 13th June, 1888.

ance to consider carefully how far the same general law can be formulated of the two cases. Now the theory of agricultural rent is perfectly precise, and, in a condition of affairs ruled solely by free and active industrial competition, would hold perfectly of the actual facts. According to this theory, rent does not enter into the price of the product; it is the price of the product that determines rent. In a perfect market there will be only one price for commodities of the same quality, and that price will be fixed by the expenses of production of the commodity under the most unfavourable conditions—by that portion of the article which is produced with greatest difficulty or from the least fertile and advantageously situated land. Such least fertile land will pay no rent, or a minimum rent which may be disregarded. But the expenses of the production there will fix the price of the product, and the more fertile or better situated land will pay a rent corresponding to its greater advantages. Were rents to be abolished tomorrow by a stroke of the pen, the abolition would but enrich the tenants of the more fertile soils. The same amount of corn and cattle would be required as before; the conditions of production would be the same in the least advantageous circumstances. These would fix the price of the product; food would not be cheaper, and wages would not be raised.

The question thus arises : Is the rent of a mine determined in the same way as the rent of a farm ? Does it therefore not enter into the price of the product at all, so that its abolition would not cheapen coal and iron, but only enrich certain mining lessees, while its confiscation would not affect mining industry any more than the confiscation of any equal amount of other private property ? Such questions may seem strange to those who agitate for the abolition of royalties or for the nationalisation of property in mines, and who are usually well acquainted with the facts of the trade, although they may not always be able to anticipate the effects of the changes they propose. Yet economists have been in the habit of answering these questions in the affirmative. Thus Ricardo, who formulated the law of rent in the way in which it is still stated, applies that law without distinction to mines as well as farms. "Mines, as well as land," he says, "generally pay " a rent to their owner; and this rent, as well as the rent of land, " is the effect, and never the cause, of the high value of their " product. . . The return for capital from the poorest mine " paying no rent, would regulate the rent of all the other pro- " ductive mines. This mine is supposed to yield the ordinary " profits of stock. All that the other mines produce more than " this, will necessarily be paid to the owners for rent. Since this " principle is precisely the same as that which we have already

" laid down respecting land, it will not be necessary to enlarge
" on it."[30]   With equal distinctness Bagehot says, "The produc-
" tion of valuable things on the surface of the ground is exactly
" like the extraction of valuable things from beneath that surface ;"
and "it is the worst mine which can in the long run be kept going
" that in the long run determines the price of the produce."[31]

Now it is easy to see that the "worst mine" cannot "in the
" long run be kept going," nor can any mine be kept going "in the
" long run." In this obvious particular, at any rate, the mine differs
from the farm. Mines differ in their fertility and advantages of
situation just as farms do. The price of mineral products will be
regulated by their expenses of production in the worst mines
which require to be worked to meet the demand, just as the price
of agricultural produce is regulated by the expenses of production in the "worst farms" which require to be cultivated. But,
because the "worst farm" pays no rent, it does not follow that the
"worst mine" pays none. The worst mine (or any mine) cannot
be kept going "in the long run ;" the worst farm can. It improves
by being cultivated, if cultivated in workman-like manner, or at
least does not deteriorate. Landlords would rather have such land
cultivated than lie waste. It may be said therefore to pay no rent.
But a mine deteriorates by being worked. The landlord would
rather have his mine lie idle and unopened unless he is to receive
some distinct gain from its being worked. Mining operations do
not contribute towards the amenity of the neighbourhood, and by
allowing his mine to be worked, the landlord loses a possible future
source of income. It is evident therefore that the least fertile
mine worked pays a rent. The landlord will not even work it
himself, unless he looks for a return in the shape of rent. He will
rather invest his capital in some other undertaking, and meanwhile
preserve the beauty of his neighbourhood, and wait for the turn of
trade which may give value to the mine. Hence as mines deteriorate by being worked, the landlord will only let them at a rent
bearing some proportion to the amount of deterioration they suffer.
Even the least fertile mine worked will pay a rent of this kind,
and this rent will enter into the price of the product.

The case may be put still more clearly, if we adopt the method
of explaining the law of rent used in James Mill's "Elements of
" Political Economy," and in Marshall's "Economics of Industry."
The postulate of a least fertile land paying no rent may seem
difficult of verification when we come to fit our theory to facts.
But the theory admits of statement without this postulate. The
tenant of a farm, who has capital at command, will apply succes-

[30] " Principles of Political Economy and Taxation," chap. iii, " Works," p. 45.
[31] " Economic Studies," p. 127.

sive portions or "doses" of capital to the land until (owing to diminishing returns) the last portion of capital thus applied will only just return in commodities the expenses of their production. This portion therefore will pay no rent. But the previous doses of capital which yield in commodities more than the expenses of production of these commodities will pay that surplus as rent. On every farm, therefore, we may say, there is a margin or fringe of produce—that, namely, which is the result of the last application of capital and labour to the land, the application which it is only just worth the farmer's while to make—which pays no rent. But, in the case of mines, this does not hold. There the last portion of capital and labour applied (or rather its product) pays as large a share of rent as any other. The last ton of coal or ironstone raised pays the same royalty as the first. The royalty system thus prevents the theory of rent from holding true of mines as it does of agricultural land; and the royalty system itself is rendered necessary by the fundamental difference between a farm and a mine, that the latter is, while the former is not, deteriorated by working.

This is sometimes expressed by saying that in the case of mines a certain quantity of raw material is removed, and that the royalty is simply a payment for this raw material. No objection need be taken to this mode of statement. It is adopted to avoid the error made by Ricardo and others in applying the economic theory of rent to mines. But we must not be content with the statement that the royalty is simply a payment for raw material removed. It is necessary to ask what determines the amount of this payment and its variations. The economic theorist may answer that, in the long run, in this as in other cases, the price will be determined by the expenses of production. But what we must note is this: In the market, mineral of the same quality sells at a definite sum. But this same mineral as it lay in the bowels of the earth was sold to *entrepreneurs* at very different sums. The theory of royalties must show what determines the difference. The higher royalties are undoubtedly due to the peculiar advantages which particular mines have over the mines which can just be worked at a profit, in the same way as the rent of good farms exceeds that of the "worst farm" worked. So far the "rent theory" holds; so far, but no farther. For while the worst farm (which suffers no deterioration by working) pays no rent, the "worst mine" goes down in value with every ton of mineral removed, and therefore does pay a rent or royalty. For every ton of mineral worked, payment has therefore to be made; and the obligation to pay this charge affects the price at which it is possible for the producer (say from the "worst mine") to sell the produce. This cannot be treated (as it may be in the case of agricultural land) as a minimum rent, which for purposes of theory may be regarded as zero. Even a halfpenny a ton would amount to a considerable royalty rent, which could not be disregarded for the purposes of a theory however abstract. And it need hardly be said that halfpenny royalties are not met with in English mines. We are entitled to conclude therefore that to some extent royalty does enter into price. The question is, to what extent?

The answer to this question presents no theoretical difficulty. The price of the product depends upon the expense of production in the least advantageous circumstances—in the " worst mine," that is, which requires to be worked to meet the demand. Such worst mine pays a royalty, and this royalty payment enters into expenses of production, and goes to determine price. Royalties on other mines of the same kind so far as they exceed this *minimum royalty* (as it may be called) do not enter into expenses of production, and therefore do not affect price. For purposes of illustration, we may suppose that 4*d.* a ton is the minimum royalty for coal or ironstone. I cannot vouch for the accuracy of this supposition, but I do not think it will be found far from the mark. I do not know of any royalty on ironstone (even in Cleveland) that goes below 4*d.*; and, although I have come across two leases in which the royalty on coal is less, one of these at any rate seems exceptional. It is in the lease of a Yorkshire mine containing ironstone, coal, limestone, and building stone, and for the three last of these minerals the royalty is 3*d.* per ton (of 22½ cwt.). In the other lease referred to, the royalty is 3¾*d.* per ton (of 20 cwt.). I do not think however that in supposing, for purppses of illustration, that the minimum royalty is 4*d.* a ton on both coal and ironstone, we shall be making an assumption very wide of the fact.

For every ton of coal or ironstone raised and brought to market, we suppose the landlord to receive 4*d.* at least—much more from the more fertile mines, not less from the worst mines. The worst mine pays 4*d.* for every ton it puts in the market. The price of the produce must therefore in the long run be sufficient to return this 4*d.* to the mine worker, as well as his other expenses of production. This sum of 4*d.* will therefore enter into price as a part of the expenses of production. But take another and more fertile mine, producing mineral of the same quality, where the royalty is (let us say) 8*d.* Does this royalty also enter into price? The answer must be that in this case half of the royalty (what corresponds to the minimum royalty) enters into price, and that the other half does not, being a payment to the landlord for the special advantages of this particular mine. Were 4*d.* struck off this second royalty, the *entrepreneur* would not reduce the price of his product nor raise the wages of his workmen. The price would be already fixed by the less favoured mines which had formerly paid 4*d.*, and which could just be worked at a profit. Unless for the purposes of driving these out of the field, he would not reduce prices. The reduction of royalty would simply have the effect of enabling the *entrepreneur* to keep 4*d.* a ton in his own pocket, which he would otherwise have had to transfer to the landlord's. If, therefore, by Act of Parliament or otherwise, we could deduct 4*d.* a ton from every existing royalty, the produce would be cheapened by that amount. If, by the same authority, we were to forbid the charging a higher royalty than 4*d.*, neither prices would be lowered nor wages raised, but only the lessees of the more favoured mines would be enriched.[32]

. The limits within which this theory correctly expresses the facts will depend upon the extent to which the competition between royalty owners and employers is equal, unrestrained, and effective. Now it is evident that if competition is in any way restricted here, the restriction is of a different kind from that which we find in the contracts for farm rents. In the mining industry the tenant is at least the equal economically of the landlord, and well able to take care of his own interests. Nor is there any hereditary sentiment between the contracting parties or any social custom to interfere with either in the active pursuit of his own gain. There are, however, circumstances in the physical conditions under which mining is carried on which make it impossible for us to expect anything more than the most rough correspondence between the theoretical or competitive and the actual rent. These circumstances are chiefly three: the impossibility of predicting the future developments of trade and the consequent demand for coal and iron; the comparative ignorance of the yield of the mine and of the difficulty and expense of working it before operations have actually begun; and the custom of long leases rendered necessary by the large initial expenditure required for sinking the mine. Thus in earlier days ignorance of the great developments in store for the iron and coal trades led to long leases at a low rent or royalty; while in 1872 and 1873 the expectation of a long continued period of brisk trade and high prices led to mines being taken and worked at royalty rents which the

[32] Yet a project not unlike this equalisation of royalties sometimes seems to find favour. Thus a speaker at the conference of the South Wales Colliery Workmen's Federation, on 12th June, 1888, while holding that "no justice could be done "without abolishing royalties," would allow the landlords a penny a ton (irrespective of the value of the mineral or of the land) as compensation for damage done to the surface.—"South Wales Daily News," 13th June, 1888.

lessees soon found it impossible to pay. The long lease is in its origin simply a protection of the tenant against "disturbance" and the loss of his fixed capital; its effect has been to enrich those employers who entered into their agreements before the period of inflated prices, and to ruin those who took leases during that period. Perhaps "in the long run," as the economists say, the rent charged will be the competitive or economic rent; but it may be doubted whether English coal and iron will hold out for a run long enough to give the theory a fair chance of holding true. There does not seem at present to be any exact correspondence between the amount of rent and the advantages of the mine. Even in a new district like Cleveland, the good mines, we are told,[33] were early taken up, and those who came into the trade or district afterwards had to be content with inferior mines at a rent which competition had often forced up abnormally. Probably the general proposition holds true that the rent is (considering their advantages) much lighter in the good mines with their nominally high royalties, than in the poor mines with their nominally low royalties. " Better pay half-a-crown a ton at Eston," remarked a Middlesborough ironmaster, " than get for nothing at all some of the " mines that are actually being worked." A poor mine, like bad land, is "dear at any rent."

On the whole, it would seem that the rich mines are usually in possession of the large capitalists. This result is arrived at in two ways. Those who have obtained leases of the more fertile and more favourably situated mines are the stuff out of which large capitalists are made; and in competition with others, the great capitalists are better able to make terms and thus to obtain the richer mines for themselves. The landlord prefers to deal with a rich man who is sure to be able to meet his engagements, than with a poor man who may be ruined by an adverse turn of trade. Hence the tendency for the good mines to be monopolised by the large capitalists. Now it is the large capitalists who have the chief say in determining prices. The market prices are usually the prices at which they can be induced to work; and the smaller men have to struggle to keep up with them. It would seem therefore that although the theoretical or "normal" price is said to be fixed by expenses of production in the poorest mines, the actual or "market" price is determined by a competition in which the workers of these poorer mines have but little say. But although the workers of the poorer mines do not fix the market price, their existence is an index of the average about which the price oscillates. The fact that these poorer mines (at a low nominal royalty) can be worked, and that the smaller capitalists are able to go on working

---

[33] *Cf.* Percy, " Mine Rents," pp. 20 and 21.

them, forms a test or measure of the conditions of possible profitable production. The fact that the poorer mines continue going
shows that the royalties on them bring them to just about the
level of profitable working. It is of course to be borne in mind
that the supposition that the poorer mines are generally in the
hands of the small capitalists is not put forward as holding true
strictly or universally. Poor mines are often taken (along with
other and richer mines) by great capitalists, who would certainly
not sink their money in them without good ground for thinking
the concern profitable.

Although, therefore, day by day, in actual trade, it is not the
expenses of production on the worst mine that fix prices, and
although it is rather prices that determine what mines can continue
working, yet the expenses on the worst mines are nevertheless a
measure of average prices. They are not the mechanism which
drives trade, but they are the dial which records the successive
stages in its progress. The royalty paid upon them, what I have
called the minimum royalty, is a part of the expenses of production, and thus, if not from day to day, yet year by year, is a factor
in price. The additional advantages of the better mines either go
to the landlord in the shape of a royalty in excess of the minimum,
or they remain with the employer who has had the good fortune,
or the skill, to get his lease on favourable terms.

My conclusion is, therefore, that the English system of private
ownership of minerals raises the price by the amount of the
minimum royalty : which, according to the rough guess I have
ventured upon, is about 4*d.* a ton for both coal and ironstone ; not
more than that sum, if my information is correct, and probably
not much, if at all, less.

### V.—*The Effect of Royalties on International Competition.*

I have now to inquire how far this burden puts English trade
at a disadvantage in presence of foreign competition.

It has been already pointed out that in the chief mining
countries of the continent—in France, Germany, and Spain—the
owner of the surface has no *primâ facie* claim, as he has in Great
Britain and the United States, to the minerals underneath. The
subsoil is regarded as either the property of the State, or as *res
nullius*, until the State has conceded to some one the right to
work it ; and then it becomes his property on the conditions laid
down by the State.[34] This concession may be granted to anyone

---

[34] Except in the case of certain of the old private royalty rights in Germany,
which are maintained under the present law. *Cf.* " Reports of Her Majesty's
" Representatives Abroad on Mining Rents and Royalties." Commercial, No. 7
(1887), p. 9 f.

who makes application for it or "denounces" the mine. In France and Spain, and, I believe, in Germany also, it is not even necessary that he should be a citizen of the country; he may be a foreigner. The development of mining industry and the conditions of trade have thus brought about quite a different state of affairs from that which was contemplated in 1789, when mineral property was first nationalised in France. At that time the intention was that mines were to be owned and worked by the people of the district, for their own benefit and that of the country, with the assistance of experts provided by the State. " When they (the inspectors " and engineers) shall have discovered mines or fossils of whatever " nature which can be worked with advantage, they shall invite," it was at first provided, "the proprietors of the land to work them, " or, in their default, the nearest inhabitants of the district: they " shall encourage and aid them with their advice, and procure " them all the facilities in their power."[35] Now, however, the mines may be worked by the first discoverer or first comer, whether citizen or foreigner.

The concession gives full possession of the property to the *concessionaire.* In France "an act of concession confers a right of " perpetual property in a mine, and gives to the mine with its " buildings, engines, pits, galleries, houses, materials, tools, and " utensils, the quality of real property (*immeuble*)."[36] So in Germany : "The permit, the so-called *Bergwerkseigenthum*, which " issues from the leasing in conformity with the mining law, of the " minerals taken away from the possession of the owner of the " soil, conveys the absolute right, in conformity with the mining " law, to work for the mineral mentioned in the license, within the " prescribed area; and to erect, above and below ground, any " apparatus necessary thereto. The right is, therefore, a peculiar " one, and one differing essentially from the general conceptions " of personal property, which should rather be classed as real " property."[37] The law of Spain is similar. "The Spanish " Government offers every facility for mining enterprise. The " subsoil belongs to the nation; any person or company, whether " foreign or Spanish, can register a claim or *denuncio* at the " Government Mining Office, situated in the capital of such " province. After the lapse of time prescribed by law, the engineer " deputed by the Government lays off the claim on the ground, " and after payment of dues the title deeds are delivered. The " denouncer of the 'claim' thus becomes possessed of all its " mineral wealth, and has a right to start workings, expropriating

[35] Arrête du Comité de Salut Public du 18 messidor.—" Journal des Mines de " la Republique," No. 1er, Vendemiaire de l'an III, p. 107.
[36] " Reports on Mining Rents," p. 5.     [37] Ibid., p. 8.

" the surface owner, should he refuse to sell his ground at a fair
" price. Starting workings is not necessary, and the owner can
" allow his concession to remain unworked any length of time.
" The smallest claim laid off is a square of 100 metres side (10,000
" square metres)." [38]

Upon this concession certain charges are made by the Government. The *concessionaire* has of course to pay the technical and legal expenses incurred in marking off the claim and making out the lease. Besides this, certain payments (settled by authority of Government) have to be made to the owner of the surface. In Spain this seems only to bo in compensation for the use of, or injury done to, the surface. The same is, in the great majority of cases, true of Germany. In several districts, however, rents have to be paid to the owners of the soil. " Such is, for instance, the " arrangement in Anhalt in the brown coal mines, where the " owner of the soil is entitled to 6 per cent. of the gross produce, " independently of the mining royalty paid by the works to the " State." [39]

In France the landlord's dues are sometimes much more considerable. The *concessionaire* has to buy the surface, of the use of which the owner is deprived, or which is rendered unfit for cultivation, for a sum which is not to exceed double the value of the land before the occupation. Besides this a *redevance tréfoncière* has to be paid to the owner of the surface for the concession; and in some cases this rent is proportional to the gross yield of the mine. " According to the calculation of a " practical engineer, the *redevance tréfoncière* habitually paid " [on the coal mines] in the basin of the Loire in 1863 varied " according to depth between 50 c. and 70 c. ($4\frac{3}{4}d.$ to $6\frac{3}{4}d.$) per " ton, which is not much less than the charge of 6*d.* to 10*d.* per " ton common as royalty in England. In the basin of the " Aveyron, according to M. Dupont, the *redevance tréfoncière* " has been set for the collieries of Aubin, Cransac, Negrin, and " Ruhles at 1 c. per hectolitre (2·75 English bushels) of coal, " for depths of less than 50 metres, $\frac{1}{2}$ c. for depths down to 100 " metres, and $\frac{1}{4}$ c. for depths greater than 100 metres. This, in " practice, is much less than the *redevance* in the basin of the " Loire. In iron mines the proportional *redevance* varies from " 10 c. (1*d.*) to 8 c. ($\frac{3}{4}d.$) per metric quintal " (*i.e.*, 100 kilograms, or 220$\frac{1}{2}$ lbs.). More frequently however the *redevance* is a fixed sum per hectare (2$\frac{1}{2}$ acres). And although exceptional cases are quoted in which " they are as high as 300 frs. per hectare (equal to

[38] J. Allan, in tho " Iron and Coal Trades Review," 14th October, 1887; *cf.* " Reports on Mining Rents," p. 32.
[39] " Reports on Mining Rents," p. 10.

" 5*l.* 6*s.* 5*d.* per acre)—salt mines de l'Est—or 50 frs. per hectare
" (equal to 17*s.* 7¾*d.* per acre—manganese ores of Romanêche,"
the great majority of them are for the merely nomiual sums of
5 to 10 c. per hectare.[40]

In addition to these payments to the landlord—in some cases
almost as heavy in France as the English royalty, but for the
most part of merely nominal amount—an additional payment has
to be made to the State. This is smallest in Spain, where the
sole object of the mining regulations seems to be to attract capital
to the country.[41] No payment is levied in proportion to the output.
The only charge made is a small annual sum varying with the
surface extent.[42] The French Government charges a yearly rent
of 10 frs. per square kilometre, and in addition a royalty of 5 per
cent. on the *net* produce, or profit, of the mine.[43] In Germany the
charge made on coal is 2 per cent. on the *gross* value of the output.
The purpose of recent laws " is the gradual reduction of the tithe
" originally chargeable, by the mining law common to Germany and
" Prussia, on all mines leased by the State, and the conversion of
" it into a 2 per cent. charge on the value, at the time of the output,
" of the produce taken from the mine, and the conversion of the
" mining taxes levied on the left bank of the Rhine, under the
" regulations of the French Mining Law of 21st April, 1810, into
" the said 2 per cent. charge on the gross value of the output."
On iron ore the German Government charges no royalty.[44]

Sir Lowthian Bell illustrates the above by saying, of Germany,
that if the selling price of coal is 6*s.* a ton, the royalty will be less
than 1½*d.*; and of France, that if the profits of the manufacturer
of pig are 2*s.* a ton, he will pay less than 1¼*d.* a ton on the coal and
ore used in the manufacture.[45] These facts may be made clearer
by the subjoined Table C:—

[40] "Reports on Mining Rents," pp. 4 and 5.

[41] The success of the regulations may be indicated by the fact that 40,000,000*l.*
of British capital is said to be invested, directly or indirectly, in the mines of
Spain and Portugal.—"Times," 21st December, 1887.

[42] According to Sir Clare Ford's return, "mines measuring 300 by 200 metres
" horizontally pay an annual royalty to Government of 75 pesetas (3*l.*); mines
" measuring 500 by 330 metres, 50 pesetas (2*l.*)."—"Reports on Mining Rents,"
p. 32. Probably the figures have been transposed. The Spanish Government
offers great facilities to mining industry, but would hardly be likely to make the
charge high in proportion as the concession is small.

[43] "Reports on Mining Rents," p. 6.

[44] Ibid., p. 8.

[45] "Principles of the Manufacture of Iron and Steel," p. 609.

TABLE C.—*Royalties Payable to the State in Foreign Countries.*

| | On Coal. | | On Ironstone. | | Estimated Royalty Charge per Ton of Pig Iron.* |
| --- | --- | --- | --- | --- | --- |
| | Percentage. | Estimated Charge per Ton.* | Percentage. | Estimated Charge per Ton.* | |
| Germany.... | 2% of output | 1½d. | Nil | Nil | 6d. |
| France........ | 5% of profit | 1¼d. | 5% of profit | 1¼d. | 8d. |
| Belgium .... | 2½%   ,, | −⅝d. | — | 4¾d. to 2s.† | 1s. 3d. to 4s.‡ |
| Spain ........ | Nil | Nil | Nil | Nil | Nil |

\* *Cf.* Sir L. Bell's "Principles of the Manufacture of Iron and Steel," p. 610.

† Payable to the surface owner. The working of the Belgian ironstone is now discontinued.

‡ *Cf.* the preceding note.

N.B.—The above are the royalties payable by the *concessionaire* to the State, and do not include the royalties paid by the *entrepreneur* to the *concessionaire.* Nor do they take account of the exceptional cases in which high royalties have to be paid to the owner of the surface, or of the payments made to compensate him for the destruction of the surface (also excluded from Table B). Royalties in the United States vary from nothing at all to 6s. or 7s. per ton of pig iron. *Cf.* Sir L. Bell's evidence before the Royal Commission on the Depression of Trade, Q. 3566.

In these dues to the State and to the owner of the surface, the continental employer has to make payments similar in kind to—though, as a rule, much less in amount than—the royalties which the English mine owner pays his landlord. Yet the foreign system is not really so favourable to the employer and to the trade, as this alone might lead us to imagine. There is, indeed, a certain illusoriness about the so-called "no royalty" system to which the progress of our foreign competitors is sometimes, without due consideration, attributed. Not only have the *concessionaires* to pay the dues above described to the State and to the owner of the soil ; but in France, Germany, and Spain, competitive royalties—fixed in the same way as in England, and of similar amount—have often to be paid by the actual employer of labour. They are, indeed, not paid—as they commonly are in England—to the landlord, but to a third party, who is unknown in this country, and for whose existence the continental mining laws are responsible. By the French law of 1810, " the concession of a mine. . . creates a new " property, independent of and separate from that of the surface, " a property transmissible like any other. An act of concession " confers a right of perpetual property in a mine."⁴⁶ With some differences of detail this provision also holds in Germany and in

⁴⁶ " Reports on Mining Rents," p. 5.

Spain. The original *concessionaire* in these countries occupies very much the same position as the English landlord : with this important difference, that he has no other interest in the property than to get as much out of it as he can. He is not a lessee, but an owner, and can do what he likes with his own. The English mining lessee is usually, by the provisions of his lease, deprived of the privilege of sub-letting. But no restriction of this kind attaches to the French or German or Spanish *concessionaire.* He is not even obliged to work the mine at all; he may allow it to stand idle, or he may let it for what royalty he can get. Very commonly he does the latter. He gets the concession for nothing —or almost nothing—from the Government, and then lets it, at the highest royalty it will bring, to those who have capital and skill to work it. There is no detailed evidence, so far as I am aware, to show in what number of cases mines are worked by the original *concessionaire* himself, and in what number of cases they are let by him to the worker. But the latter method is certainly not uncommon, especially in the case of the richest mines. Thus the Orconera Company, which works the famous Bilbao mines, has not itself the concession of mining rights from the Spanish Government, but rents them at a high royalty from the original *concessionaire.* To this case Mr. Dale was probably referring in his question[47] to one of the witnesses before the recent Royal Commission on the Depression of Trade : " Would you be surprised to hear that the " royalty rents in Spain are not unusually 2*s.* a ton on hæmatite " ore ?" The witness was surprised to hear it; but as Mr. Dale is himself the Chairman of the Consett Spanish Ore Company, we may be sure that he was not speaking without accurate knowledge of the facts.

It is probable that this system of letting the working at a royalty is commoner with the *concessionaires* of the richer, than with those of the poorer mines. And, if this be the case, and if the expenses of production in the worst mines be looked on as measuring the price of the product, it will still appear that the expenses on them are, as regards rent charges, less on the continent than in England. In England, as has already been pointed out, the owners of the worst mines, being also owners of the surface, are unwilling to have the mines worked unless they return a considerable royalty. But on the continent, where the French mining law of 1810, or laws founded on it, are in force, the landlord has no power to prevent the mines from being worked ; and the *concessionaire* looks simply for such profit—usually immediate profit—as he can get. The mines just worth working will only have to pay the small State tax or royalty and the (usually nominal) dues to the

[47] Q. 2355.

landlord. These payments will enter into expenses of production, and so add to price; but they will be found to be very much less than the corresponding royalty dues on the worst English mines which are worked. It would seem, therefore, that English mining industry has a heavier burden to bear in the way of royalty than continental mining industry. The relative expenses of production in the former exceed those in the latter by the difference between the English minimum royalty and the smaller dues paid abroad. Corresponding to the higher royalties on the better mines paid to the landlord in England, there is an exactly similar royalty paid to the original *concessionaire* abroad, or else a surplus profit which the *concessionaire*—if he works the mine himself—is able to retain. It is a mistake to look upon these high royalties either here or abroad as a burden upon industry, provided they be fixed by fair competition and with sufficient knowledge of the nature of the mine and of the state of trade. In the one case the landlord, and, in the other case, the original *concessionaire*, receives the competitive or economic rent. It is true that in this country the landlords possess a valuable property which many might wish to see better distributed, and which we might think ourselves able to distribute better, if things were all to be begun over again. But it would be a perverse imitation of foreign countries, to advocate the expropriation of the landlord simply for the benefit of the adventurers encouraged by the French or Spanish system of concessions.

It may be true that the continental system, in abolishing or restricting the rights of the owner of the surface, leads to the royalties on the poorer mines being less abroad than in this country. If royalties were to be abolished in England, the product would therefore be cheapened, but not by so large an amount as is commonly supposed. This would no doubt give a certain advantage in doubtful cases to English trade, and would thus extend its operation and make employment easier to get at present, if not more regular for the future. Further, there would of course be a large additional gain from the richer mines, but this would go into the pockets of the employers.

The development of the iron trade abroad, especially in Germany, of recent years, has undoubtedly put a great additional strain upon the resources and energy of British industry. But royalties have very little to do with this keener competition. "The expansion of "the iron trade as referring to steel in Germany," says Mr. I. T. Smith in the passage already quoted of his evidence before the Royal Commission on the Depression of Trade, "has not been a "question of royalty during the last four or five years, so much as "of the discovery of a process by which their own ore can be "converted into steel." [*]

[*] Q. 2450.

## VI.—*Proposed Reforms.*

The preceding discussion of the incidence of royalties, and their effect on price and international competition, will enable us to understand better what would be the real effect of the various reforms of the English royalty system which have been suggested from different quarters.

There is much more agreement in the trade as to the defects of the present system than as to any practical proposals for relief or reform. At the same time, reforms of various kinds are confidently demanded; and among the reformers it is not surprising to find many persons of opinion that the complete subversion of the present system is called for. But it is not always clearly seen that there are two different ways in which the present system might be done away with. Property in minerals might be transferred from individuals to the State—nationalised, that is to say: and that is one proposal for total reform. But the present system might be subverted in another way—by forbidding any payment for the privilege of working mines, that is to say, by the abolition of royalties. The two proposals are not always distinguished, and the common arguments against royalties generally leave it in doubt whether it is their nationalisation or abolition that is desired, and held up as the panacea for industrial distress. It must be admitted that the nationalisation of minerals might conceivably be followed by the abolition of royalties, and would probably be followed at least by new methods for levying them. Yet for a clear understanding of the question, the two proposals must be kept distinct.

I do not propose to enter at length into the arguments for either the nationalisation or abolition of royalties, so far as that means the confiscation of private property. The demand for such confiscation seems to me to be only a part of the larger demand for the confiscation of landed property, and that again to be a part of the still wider claim now frequently made for the confiscation of all private property in the instruments of production. The argument sometimes used that the landlord has no right to the minerals, seeing "he did not put them there," can impose upon no one who has given any serious attention to the basis of political and proprietory rights. It may be true, indeed, that the Crown once possessed more extensive rights to minerals than it now does. But, whatever its claims have been, no evidence can be produced that it was ever regarded as the beneficiary owner of mines any more than of lands. Even the mysterious Scotch Act of 1592, which remained so long unprinted and unknown, has never been interpreted as giving the Crown a right to all minerals,[49] however plain its assertion of the royal claim may appear to the lay mind. We may indeed regret that so much valuable mineral property has passed into private hands, when a different law of ownership might, at one time, have preserved it for the people as a whole without injustice. But a long period of vested rights, confirmed by statutory enactments, has made minerals as much private property as the surface of the soil, or indeed as moveable estate. Without an arbitrary interference with private right, they could not at present be assumed by the State, except by buying out the present owners; and to do this now would probably prove to be a bad investment of the national funds. Besides, it must be remembered that the nationalisation of minerals need have no effect upon mining lessees or upon the price of minerals; it would merely change the owners. The lessees would have to pay a royalty to the State instead of to a private individual; and the mining industry need be no more affected by the transference than any other industry in the country. It is true that the State, in becoming the owner of minerals, might introduce a reformed method of assessing and levying the royalties and other payments that are at present borne by the lessee. But State ownership is by no means a necessary pre-condition of State regulation; and, if a case can be made out for the interference of the State, such interference might be introduced here—as it has already been introduced in other departments—without doing away with private ownership.

The cry for abolition is, in some respects, more intelligible than the proposal to nationalise minerals. When any institution is found to be defective, "abolish it" is the easiest suggestion to make, and the readiest to find acceptance. It is the simplest reform to carry out, if we are to look only to the immediate effect, and disregard both the cause of the grievance and the ultimate result of the remedy. The first impulse is always to pull up the tares without taking thought of the danger to the wheat. A little reflection however may show that abolition is not, any more than nationalisation, the best remedy in the present case. Let us suppose, for the moment, that we had a Government with so little economic foresight as to abolish royalties—and, perhaps, so devoid of moral

[49] By this statute the right to all mines, metals, and minerals was declared to belong to the Crown; without the consent of the Crown, no private contract between the owners of the surface and lessees was recognised; and the owners of the surface were to be compelled to grant wayleaves and ground for building, with compensation for surface damage only. The Act was unknown to the earlier commentators on the law of Scotland, Stair and Mackenzie. When it has been appealed to, in more recent times, the court has decided that the Act (although it does speak generally of all mines) applies only to mines royal, being controlled by the earlier statutes.—*Cf.* Rankin, "Law of Landownership in Scotland, 1879," pp. 136 and 137.

principle as to do so without compensation. What would be the effect? Royalty payments are abolished all over the kingdom; a burden is lifted from industry; every mine is benefited—these are the obvious and immediate results; and their consequences are foretold with equal triumph: a lower price, a quickened demand, higher wages. This however is but a partial and superficial account of what would happen. It is evident, in the first place, that if every mine is benefited, they are not all benefited equally. The south Wales coal fields will receive a bonus in the way of remitted royalty of about 8*d.* or 9*d.* a ton, those of Durham and Northumberland a bonus of 4*d.* or 5*d.* a ton only. The lessees of the rich hæmatite mines of Cumberland will find that they may now retain 2*s.* a ton which they formerly had to pay in royalty; in Cleveland the lessee will be relieved to the extent of from 4*d.* to 6*d.* or 7*d.* only. The abolition of royalties would therefore mean, in the first instance, a granting of unequal privileges to different districts and different mining lessees. The existing equilibrium of trade would be disturbéd, and a new distribution of industry, with all its attendant hardships, would at once begin to take effect. The present system of mining royalties has not been in operation so long without bringing about a certain balance or equilibrium. The lessee of the rich mines has to pay a larger royalty than the lessee of the poorer mines; and it is this which enables the latter to carry on the competition with his better situated rival. Remove the royalties, and his competition will be rendered less effective at every point where the interests of the two clash. The poorer lessee will be gradually worsted and driven out of the field, while the lessee of the richer mine increases his output. The same process of disturbance will take place between different districts; and it is to the credit of the intelligence rather than of the prudence of the Northumberland Political Reform Association, that when pronouncing in favour of the abolition of royalties, they did so with their eyes open, a speaker having shown them how the slighter gain which would fall to the portion of Northumberland, in comparison with south Wales, would give the latter an advantage which might lead to the destruction of the Northumberland coal trade. Royalties may be artificial, but they have had the effect of producing a certain balance between different districts unequally favoured in the distribution of natural advantages. Rashly to disturb that balance would be to change the conditions of production, and necessitate the slow and painful process of a readjustment of industry.

Nor would the effect of abolition in lowering price and raising wages compensate for the industrial disturbance and confusion thus caused. It has been already shown that only the minimum

royalty enters into the normal price to which actual prices tend.
The abolition of royalties would reduce price by this amount; but
the remaining portion of the royalties actually paid would not go
in reducing price, but would be presented to the lessees of the
more favoured mines.    It is true that the reduction of price
actually made would lead to an increased demand, which would
have the effect of increasing wages at the same time; but this
increased demand could be met by the richer mines now freed from
the royalty burden, and would leave the poorer mines and their
lessees struggling against unwonted disadvantages — only half
understood, because felt in an expanding trade.

It has been already shown that, in spite of the easy terms on
which mining privileges are acquired on the continent, especially
in Spain, a new royalty system has grown up there, at any rate
for the better mines.   The *concessionaire* becomes the owner, and
lets his property at a royalty to a new lessee.   To the latter it
makes no difference whether payment of the royalty has to be
made to the surface owner or to an adventurer who has been
beforehand in the discovery of the mine.   A royalty is agreed upon
by private contract, and paid just as in this country.   Such is the
result of the legislation which, disregarding private right, con-
fiscated mineral property for the good of the public.   The original
*concessionaire* has been able to transfer to his own pocket the
value which an unwise law took from its former owner with the
benevolent intention of distributing it to the people.   A similar
result would follow the confiscation of mines in this country, unless
means were devised for preventing the transference of mining
privileges from one person to another.

No such drastic remedy as the nationalisation or abolition of
royalties is required by the condition of trade; nor would the
circumstances of trade allow such a remedy to work the wonders
sometimes expected of it.   The defects of our present system cannot
be summed up in the existence of royalties—which arise naturally
from the ownership of minerals in whomsoever vested—but rather
consist in certain circumstances connected with the way in which
royalties are levied.   Complaints are indeed made about the whole
system, as complaints are commonly made by everyone who has
made a bad bargain.   But the real grievances of the present
system seem to be, first, in the royalty payment remaining the same
while prices fall; secondly, in the high certain rents and the
limitation of time for working "shorts;" and thirdly, in the tonnage charges made for instroke and outstroke, shaft, and waylcave
rents.

1. In periods of brisk trade, when prices are high, the royalty
forms so small a portion of the employer's expenses as often to be

hardly felt. But, when the period of depression comes, and all the energies of the employer are occupied in reducing expenses within the lowered level of market prices, he finds that the royalty alone remains a fixed charge per ton, while wages fall, railway rates are reduced, and his own profits begin to disappear. At such periods we often find the lessees beginning to agitate for a reduction of royalties, as if they were farmers dependent upon the seasons, instead of masters of industry able to foresee and provide against the fluctuations of trade. It is perhaps natural that, in these circumstances, there should be some difficulty in obtaining reduction from the landlord. He has not shared in the extra profit of the good years, and he has difficulty in seeing why he is to be called upon to suffer in the depression of the bad years. As long as the royalty remains a fixed money payment, it must be expected to be felt with greatest severity just when the lower prices of produce make employers least able to bear it. For such a grievance the remedy is of the simplest kind. Were the royalty calculated on a sliding scale, so as to rise and fall with prices, both landlord and tenant would be gainers by the change—the landlord would receive a larger income in the good years, while, at the time of low prices, the lessee would find his royalty diminishing in proportion. In the royalties paid to the State in both France and Germany this principle is adopted: in Germany the royalty is a proportion (2 per cent.) of the gross output, in France a percentage (5 per cent.) of the net product, or of profit. The latter method of calculating the royalty is in some respects the fairer. It allows for the differences between mines in respect of their difficulty of working, thickness of strata, freedom from "troubles," and so forth. But it is open to all the objections which may be urged against a tax on profits, as a discouragement to skilful and successful business management. And in this country, with royalties in the possession of private owners, to assess them in proportion to profits would require a minute and far too inquisitorial investigation into the state of each employer's books. There are no such objections to assessing the royalties in proportion to the selling price of the mineral at the pit mouth (or perhaps, in the case of ironstone, to the selling price of pig iron).

Some such sliding scale arrangement seems coming into use in certain districts—usually as a concomitant or result of a reduction of royalties.[50] It is stated that "in Scotland the royalties on iron- "stone, and in some cases on coal, have for several years been " generally stated upon the principle of fluctuating with the price

[50] "Report of the Royal Commission on the Depression of Trade." Q. 3570—75.

" of pig iron."[51]  In Cumberland and Lancashire, where the
royalties were greatly reduced by the competition of the Bilbao
mines, sliding scales were introduced.  "In 1879," says Mr. I.
T. Smith, "we agitated for a reduction in royalties; we then
" commenced upon a sliding scale "[52]  We also hear—though this
is " a very great secret "[53]—of reduction and sliding scales in the
Northumberland and Durham coal mines.  " Almost all the coal.
" owners," says Mr. J. B. Simpson,[54] " are applying to the lessors
" to have their rents reduced, and in many instances they are
" successful, and very frequently sliding scales are introduced."
In Cleveland, I know of only one case of a sliding scale, and that
has been for long inoperative, as the lower limit of the scale is
reached when the selling price of pig iron is 45s. a ton.  In some
districts, moreover, the sliding scale has been given up after being
in operation for some time.  Mr. A. Hewlett, speaking on behalf of
the Wigan Coal and Iron Company and of the South Lancashire
and Cheshire Coal Association, says that the fluctuating royalty—
in his opinion, the best plan—has nevertheless come round to a
fixed royalty in his district.  The sliding scale was given up
" in consequence of the difficulties in the accounts; it involves
" looking into books and keeping statistics, and so on."[55]  And
yet it has been found practicable to arrange the fluctuations of
wages on this principle.  In South Staffordshire, too, payment
in proportion to the selling price was formerly the rule, but
is now very exceptional; "lessors have for many years past
" insisted on fixed royalties or payment by the foot per acre."
Only one colliery in the Cannock Chase district now pays on
the sliding scale principle.  " All the other collieries have fixed
" royalties per ton or per acre."

Until some such arrangement as that of a sliding scale is introduced we must expect a repetition of the old process.  Lessees
appeal to their landlords for reduction whenever trade is depressed
and prices are low.  The landlord naturally feels the one-sidedness
of the arrangement.  When prices were abnormally high, the lessee
never asked him to accept more than the stipulated royalty; he
only offers him less when prices fall.  Yet the landlord is often
obliged to give the reduction, lest his tenant fail, and the mine be
left idle.  It would therefore be to the landlord's advantage, as
well as for the tenant's convenience, if a sliding scale were adopted.
It is curious to observe, that while mining lessees almost always

---

[51] " Report of the Royal Commission on the Depression of Trade." *Q.*
3609.
[52] Ibid., *Q.* 2314.
[53] According to Mr. A. Hewlett, ibid., *Q.* 12,137.        [54] Ibid., *Q.* 12,353.
[55] " Report of the Royal Commission on the Depression of Trade," *Q.*
12,177—79.

seem in favour of such an arrangement, and it is the landlords who cannot be induced to agree to it, it is yet much more obviously to the advantage of the landlord than to that of the lessee. For, on the sliding scale, the landlord will receive high royalties when trade is brisk and production large, whereas when the royalties are low, production will in all probability have diminished. His income will therefore fluctuate with trade in a way it does not do at present; but the gross royalty yield of a mine will be found to be much greater than it is under the present system of fixed royalties.

2. Another custom which has hurtful effects upon the trade is the custom as to certain or dead rents, and the limitation of the period of working "shorts." "Such fixed rents," says Sir L. Bell, are "regarded as payments on account for future workings."[56] In some districts these dead rents are very much below what the mine can work.[57] In other districts this is not the case. Mr. A. Hewlett says it does not hold of Lancashire:[58] "in many leases where we "are getting coal we cannot get up the dead rent." In Cleveland it is customary for the certain rent to be calculated on the principle of being equal to the total royalty yield of the mine, divided by the number of years of the lease. At the end of the lease the mine is usually exhausted. The certain rent thus paid will often, in a single year, exceed the royalties that would be due for the mineral actually worked; and, in such cases, the payment already made in the form of certain rent is set against mineral taken away in some subsequent year. But this privilege of working "shorts" without further payment commonly lapses at fixed dates. The general custom in Cleveland is to allow a period of five years in which shorts may be worked. Owing to this limitation the lessee often pays twice over for the mineral he obtains, or pays for mineral which he never gets. "Taking our own case at the present "moment," says Mr. A. Hewlett, of the Wigan Coal and Iron Company,[59] "we have overpaid 260,000*l.* for coal to be hereafter "gotten, more than a quarter of a million, and more than an "eighth of the capital of the company." Further, to avoid the possible loss of these payments in advance, the lessee is induced to work off the "shorts" within the stipulated period, even when demand is slack, and thus to contribute to over production. He is almost forced to go on producing lest he lose the mineral he has paid for; so that the slackening of demand is prevented from having its full effect in restricting production. In these circumstances many lessees wish to claim the privilege of working shorts

---

[56] "Second Report of the Royal Commission on the Depression of Trade," Appendix I, p. 74 of pamphlet.
[57] "Report," Q. 12,358 and 12,407 (Mr. J. B. Simpson).
[58] Ibid., Q. 12,168.    [59] Ibid., Q. 12,122.

even after their lease has run out. To this perhaps there may be objections. But, at any rate, there would seem to be no good reason for not allowing shorts to be worked without additional payment during any subsequent year of the lease.

3. In the third place the royalty principle seems to be out of place when applied to the various charges made for instroke and outstroke, shaft, and wayleave. A royalty payment is justified in mines themselves, because the value of the property is diminished by every ton of mineral removed. But, in the case of the payments now under consideration, there is no such justification for introducing the royalty principle. It is true that a mine is deteriorated by the barrier which separates it from a neighbouring mine being broken through. It thus becomes liable to flooding and other dangers from which the barrier protected it, and it is only fair that the owner should be fully recompensed for the danger thus incurred. But the charges for instroke, &c., do not seem to bear any relation to this danger. It has never been made out, nor even suggested, that the damage done or threatened varies with the amount of mineral brought through the barrier along the way and up the shaft of the mine first sunk. Besides, we must remember that the lessee of this mine is by his original lease required to keep it free from water during the period of the lease; that the way along which he brings the mineral from the second mine is the way he has made; and that the shaft by which it is brought to the surface was sunk at his own expense. But the owner of the first mine is in the position of a monopolist, and is thus able to exact the utmost sum which the lessee would be willing to give rather than go without the privilege of working the second mine.

The same kind of monopoly exists when the wayleave is under or over ground not itself mined. In this case there is no question of an indefinite amount of damage to the ventilation or drainage of the mine, seeing there is no mine in the question. The land has a certain agricultural value, which will be lost by a wayleave across it, and may be endangered by a wayleave under it. But here again the owner of the way is put accidentally in possession of a monopoly. His strip of land may be the only means by which the mineral can be conveyed to a wharf or railway; and instances are on record of mines having to cease working owing to the heavy burdens of this kind which the possessor of a convenient— or the only—way seeks to impose upon the lessee.

It is, I think, clearly made out—and indeed commonly acknowledged—that it would be of the greatest advantage to the trade if royalties were assessed on a sliding scale, and if shorts could be worked during any year of the lease. There would seem also to be cases in which the trade would be greatly benefited if wayleaves, &c., could be obtained at a fair valuation. But the question arises, how are the reforms to be brought about ?

Now the two former proposals would not seem to bear prejudicially either upon the landlord or upon the lessee. The "sliding "scale" arrangement especially would seem to be distinctly for the landlord's interest, while it is undoubtedly desired by his tenants. Under the present law, however, the powers of limited owners are, in some respects, so restricted that reforms in the lease to which both the lessor and lessee might agree, cannot be carried out. To remedy this would require an extension of the legal powers of the limited owner. But even where there is no legal difficulty in the case, the vast majority of the contracting parties still hesitate to introduce the reform in mining leases which the conditions of trade call for; and, while they hesitate, or are unwilling to move, trade suffers : its fluctuations are more keenly felt; and the workmen who are no parties to the contract are those who are most affected and most injured by its defective conditions. It is the interests of this larger class involved in the contract, but having no voice in determining its provisions, and the connected interests of British trade, that can alone justify legislative interference in the matter. Perhaps it is not too late to hope that the changes in the conditions of the leases, recommended by the whole opinion of the trade, may yet be introduced without the necessity for parliamentary action. There is, at any rate, some reason for contending that the most urgent reform required from Parliament in the matter is the removal of the legal disabilities under which (by the Settled Land Act of 1882) limited owners at present stand in making such contracts.[60] It would seem probable however that further legislative action may yet be called for, in the way of prescribing the general conditions of mining leases. Such legislative interference would receive its justification from two considerations : first, from the industrial advantage to the community to be gained by the proposed modification of the method of levying royalties; and secondly, from the fact that parliamentary action was required in order to bring the change about. It would surely be no objection to such action that, in serving the interests of the community, it would not affect prejudicially the interests of individuals.

The third grievance is not, so far as I am aware, so widely felt as the other two; and the proposal made for remedying it, if enjoined by law, would involve a more serious interference with private liberty. It would take away from the owner of the soil an advantage which he has at present, when new developments of trade, or other circumstances, put him into possession of a valuable

[60] *Cf.* Mr. R. B. Haldane's speech in the House of Commons, 14th May, 1886.

monopoly. In favour of the proposed interference it might be argued that it is not an interference with free competition, but an interference with monopoly, and that it is not recommended in the interests of the lessee, but in the interest of British industry and of the workmen with whose employment the monopolist interferes. The principle of such interference has been already asserted in the case of the compulsory sale of land to railway companies; and, at the present day, the mining industry is of as great importance to the country at large as the development of railways. The conclusion to which this points is that Parliament would be justified in compelling the owners to grant wayleaves, &c., at a fair valuation of the land occupied or damaged, or of the injury done to the ventilation, drainage, &c., of the mine. The validity of such a conclusion, however, will depend upon its being shown that trade suffers, and that employment is rendered more difficult and irregular owing to the existence of the present monopolies, and the way in which they are exercised. Now cases can certainly be instanced—reference has already been made to such—in which the high royalty rent charged for a wayleave has acted injuriously upon trade. But I have not yet seen that amount of evidence that would be required to compel us to regard this as an evil so serious and widely spread as to call for the action of Parliament. The wayleave question is very much more a question between two landlords than a question between a landlord and the state of industry, or even between landlord and lessee. If landlord A is in possession of a mine the produce of which can only be got to market through the mine or across or under a field belonging to a neighbouring landlord B, who demands a penny for every ton of mineral that crosses his property, then A's mine will be less valuable to him by that same penny a ton: for, in making a contract with an *entrepreneur*, the royalty he will be able to get from him will be a penny a ton less than it would have been if landlord B had not blocked the way to the market. This reasoning, as well as the paucity of evidence on the subject, leads me to suspect that the cases in which trade and employment seem to have suffered owing to the exorbitant sums paid for wayleave are exceptional, and probably due either to want of information, or to want of full consideration, on the part of the *entrepreneur* when he entered upon his lease of the mine. To compel the granting of wayleaves at what might appear a fair valuation would thus, I fear, not have the desired effect upon trade, and would (to recur to my illustration) only have the effect of allowing landlord A to take the penny which would otherwise have gone into the pocket of landlord B.

To sum up, the reforms in the present royalty system which

the preceding discussion has shown to be desirable, might be carried out by a law providing that, in all future leases (1) the royalty charged should be a percentage of the output, and (2) there should be no restriction put on the time for working "shorts." The further proposal suggested (namely, that instroke and outstroke, shaft and wayleave rents, should be granted at a fair valuation of the land occupied or damaged, or of the injury done to the ventilation, drainage, &c., of the mine) would appear to be justified only if it can be shown that the interests affected by the charges made at present are those of the trade, and not merely or mainly the rival interests of different landlords, and that the remedy would benefit the trade, and not merely one owner at the expense of another. For the reasons already given this proposal seems to me to stand on quite a different level from the two preceding proposals, and not to have made out a case for legal enforcement.

The exact form in which any such reforms as those suggested should be carried out would, of course, be a matter for discussion by mining and legal experts. But one thing seems clear: no mining court would be necessary for putting them into effect; nor does there seem to be, in the defects of the present system, any sufficient reason for transferring the assessment of royalties from private agreement to the decision of such a court.

HARRISON AND SONS, PRINTERS IN ORDINARY TO HER MAJESTY, ST. MARTIN'S LANE.